T0011655

PALEONTOLOGY

ACTIVITY Book

Written by Jenny Jacoby

Illustrated by
The Boy Fitz Hammond

FOR YOUNG READERS

Racehorse for Young Readers books may be purchased in bulk at special discounts for sales promotions, corporate gifts, fund-raising or education purposes. Special editions can also be created to specifications. For details, contact the Special Sales Department at Skyhorse Publishing, 307 West 36th Street, 11th Floor, New York, NY 10018 or info@skyhorsepublishing.com.

Racehorse for Young Readers™ is a pending trademark of Skyhorse Publishing, Inc.®, a Delaware corporation.

Visit our website at www.skyhorsepublishing.com.

Please follow our publisher Tony Lyons on Instagram @tonylyonsisuncertain

ISBN
978-1-63158-726-9

10 9 8 7 6 5 4 3 2 1

Design and art direction by
Vicky Barker

Manufactured in China,
January 2024

This product conforms
to CPSIA 2008

WHAT IS Paleontology?

Paleontology is the study of ancient life—so ancient, in fact, that humans were not around yet to write anything down. To study ancient life, we have to look for clues fossilized in the rocks and ground below us. Ancient life forms can be as tiny as microscopic bacteria or as huge as a diplodocus!

Paleontology is a long word because it comes from three ancient Greek words: "palaios" meaning "ancient," "ontos" meaning "life," and "ology" meaning "study." It's a tricky spelling but not too hard to say: pay-lee-ont-olo-jee.

WHAT IS STEM?

STEM stands for "science, technology, engineering, and mathematics." These four areas are closely linked, and can be used to study and make sense of our world. We need to use scientific techniques to study the world and uncover some of the secrets about ancient life. Paleontologists use technology to help their research too!

Science

Technology

Engineering

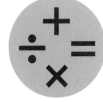
Math

PALEONTOLOGY TOOLS

Paleontologists want to know what life was like in the ancient past—that's anything more than 12,000 years ago. But because we can't time-travel, the best way to find out is by looking for things that have lasted thousands of years right through to today. Almost nothing can live that long, but luckily some things become preserved in rock as fossils—and even luckier still, some people discover those fossils.

Paleontologists use special tools to find fossils and carefully dig them out.

Tweezers

Some fossils might be so tiny that they are best picked out with hand-held tweezers.

Hard hat

Lots of places where fossils are found have loose rocks that could fall and hurt your head, so fossil hunters need to wear a hard hat.

Goggles

These are very important for protecting your eyes from any small pieces of flying rock.

Spade

Some fossils might be in softer ground, which is easier to get into with a spade than a hammer.

Field lens

Like a portable magnifying glass, this helps you to look at detail or very small fossils.

Pick

The sharp, pointed end is good for breaking up softer rocks.

Chisel

Big rocks and boulders can be broken up by hitting a wide chisel into a crack in the rock, using a hammer. Smaller chisels are good for getting a fossil out of a rock.

Notebook and pen

To record when and where fossils were found, and what the ground was like.

Hammer

These come in different shapes and sizes and their job is to break rocks!

4

Help this paleontologist find their way to the fossil dig, picking up all of their equipment on the way. Use the checklist to make sure they collect everything!

- Goggles and hard hat
- Pick
- Chisel
- Hammer
- Field lens
- Notebook and pen

Answer on page 30.

START HERE

FORMING FOSSILS

Fossils are the remains of ancient life preserved in rock. Fossils take millions of years to form and they only happen very rarely, when the conditions are exactly right.

How fossils are made

1. When an animal or plant dies, it might get buried by mud, ash, or sand (sediment). The soft parts soon rot away, leaving the skeleton.

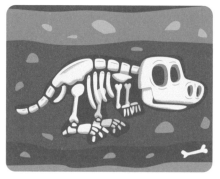

2. Over time, new layers of sediment build up, and the heavy weight pressing down eventually turns the ground around the skeleton to rock.

3. Water slowly trickles through the rock and into the bones, leaving behind mineral crystals that turn the bones to stone.

4. Sometimes, water washes away the skeleton completely and the mineral crystals fill the space, creating a cast fossil.

5. The slow movement of the land, plus weathering from wind and rain, can gradually bring the fossils closer to the surface again. This makes it more likely that paleontologists will find them.

Some fossils, called "trace fossils," are casts of a behavior rather than a body. For example, a footprint cast in mud could become a fossil that would tell us how a creature moved across land.

Add a fossil in this rock for the paleontologist to find.
You can draw the skeleton of an animal you like, or make
up an animal or plant that hasn't been discovered yet!
Don't forget to fill in the paleontologist's notes.

FIELD NOTES

Name of animal/plant: ....

Location: ....

Special features: ....

....

WHERE CAN WE FIND DINOSAURS?

Dinosaurs lived on Earth for around 180 million years. In the time of the first dinosaurs, there was just one big block of land, called Pangaea. Over millions of years, the land broke up and formed the continents we know today.

Dinosaurs lived almost everywhere on Earth. Their fossils have been found anywhere that the conditions were right and the land has worn away enough for the fossils to poke through.

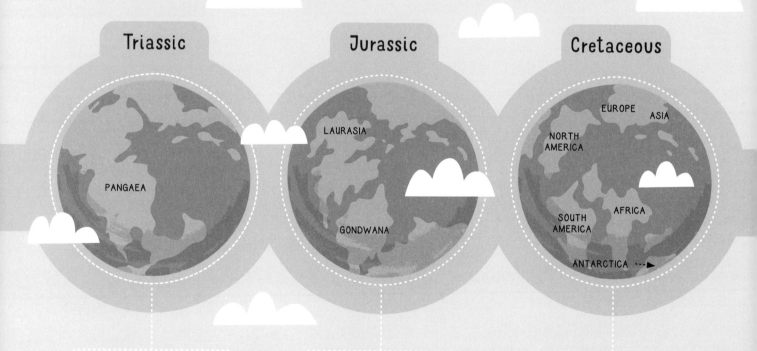

Triassic

PANGAEA

Jurassic

LAURASIA

GONDWANA

Cretaceous

EUROPE
ASIA
NORTH AMERICA
SOUTH AMERICA
AFRICA
ANTARCTICA - - -▶

252—201 million years ago: Pangaea was a C-shaped block of land.

201—145 million years ago: Pangaea broke into two blocks, called Laurasia and Gondwana. The climate was hot and humid.

145—66 million years ago: The land kept on separating.

Velociraptor

_ S _ _

Spinosaurus

A _ _ _ _ _ A

Argentinosaurus

S _ U _ _
_ _ER _ _ A

Fill in the missing letters to find out where each of these dinosaur fossils has been found. Then draw an arrow to the correct places on the map. Answers on page 30.

NORTH AMERICA

EUROPE

ASIA

AFRICA

SOUTH AMERICA

AUSTRALIA/ NEW ZEALAND

Iguanodon

_ U _ _ P _

Triceratops

_ _ _ _ T _
_ _ _ R _ _ A

Muttaburrasaurus

A _ _ _ R _ L _ _ /
N _ W
Z _ _ L _ N _

LEARNING FROM FOSSILS

If only we could talk to fossils! They can't answer all our questions but with careful study there's a lot they can teach us.

How can we tell how old a fossil is?

How can we know what the animal looked like from a pile of bones?

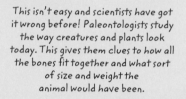

Where you find a fossil can tell you something about when it lived. That's because sedimentary rock builds up slowly over a very long time. This means that the layers closer to the surface were laid down more recently than the layers lower down. So, how far through the layers a fossil is found is a good guide to how old it is.

This isn't easy and scientists have got it wrong before! Paleontologists study the way creatures and plants look today. This gives them clues to how all the bones fit together and what sort of size and weight the animal would have been.

1.

2.

How can we tell what their life was like?

The condition a bone is found in can tell us a lot about what the animal's life was like. Some T. rex skulls show tooth marks! For the teeth to have marked the bone, the bite must have been very powerful, so paleontologists think T. rexes probably bit each other when fighting.

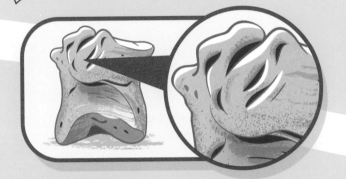

Scars can even tell us if a wound was bad enough to kill the dinosaur or if it was able to heal. If a scar has a smooth edge, it's a sign that the bone started healing while the dinosaur was alive. But if a scar has a sharp, rough edge, it's a sign that the dinosaur died soon after the break.

Can we tell what animals ate?

Sometimes paleontologists even find fossilized poo! This is called "coprolite" and by looking at it closely with a microscope we can tell what the dinosaur ate.

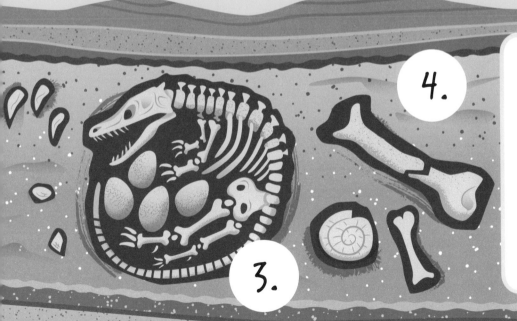

4.

Which of these fossils show that the dinosaur . . .

A . . . broke a bone and died?

B . . . was bitten in a fight?

C . . . needed to poo when it died?

D . . . looked after its eggs?

Answers on page 30.

3.

DINOSAUR SECRETS

There are some things fossils can't tell us, because as animals and plants are replaced by stone their original colors and patterns are lost. Did it have feathers or fur, or did its appearance change over its life? We can't tell any of that from a fossil either!

Because we can't know for sure what dinosaurs looked like, you can have fun designing the appearance of these below!

13

THE OLDEST FOSSILS

It takes millions of years for an organism to become a fossil. But some fossils show evidence of life *billions* of years ago!

Some of the earliest life forms on Earth were made of just one single cell. It's hard enough looking for fossils of huge dinosaurs—imagine trying to find a fossil of a cell so small it can only be seen with a microscope!

Cyanobacteria, which are each just one single cell, can group together in layers. These build up to make rock-like structures called **stromatolites**. Some of the oldest fossils we have found are stromatolites that are more than 3 billion years old! These are a record of the earliest life on Earth.

The oldest animals we have found in fossils are **trilobites**. These underwater animals looked a bit like swimming woodlice, and lived about 500 million years ago.

The world's oldest insect —400 million years old!— is called **rhyniognatha**.

The oldest known fungus, which lived 440 million years ago, is called **tortotubus**.

Something like **seaweed** lived 1.56 billion years ago.

The names of some of the oldest fossils are hidden in this word search. Can you find them? Answers on page 31.

cyanobacteria
stromatolite
trilobite
fossil

rhyniognatha
tortotubus
seaweed

y	f	o	s	s	a	g	l	f	e
k	t	k	l	t	y	i	l	r	t
c	y	a	n	r	s	a	r	u	r
a	r	a	t	s	c	n	a	i	i
b	h	b	o	m	i	n	i	y	l
t	y	f	u	s	b	i	r	e	r
d	n	d	e	e	w	a	e	s	u
n	i	n	m	a	s	i	t	u	s
f	o	t	x	o	t	h	c	r	r
l	g	h	r	t	r	k	a	v	t
e	n	i	d	i	o	o	b	p	o
w	a	c	p	c	m	d	o	z	r
a	t	m	s	o	a	e	n	c	t
e	h	t	z	s	t	v	a	q	o
s	a	t	a	j	o	i	y	o	t
m	t	m	r	v	l	a	c	x	u
a	e	q	u	a	i	r	r	a	b
h	r	h	y	t	t	k	j	d	u
i	s	o	d	e	e	o	m	i	s
t	r	i	l	o	b	i	t	e	r
q	s	b	d	r	i	m	e	p	m

WHAT DID DINOSAURS DO?

We can guess how dinosaurs behaved by looking at fossils to see how their bodies were built. Fossils show dinosaurs fought, made a lot of noise, and had to defend themselves against attackers. They also lived in groups and looked after their babies.

Parasaurolophus
had a curved, hollow crest on its head. Paleontologists think this was used like a trumpet to make loud noises to communicate with its herd or scare off predators.

Pachycephalosaurus
had such a big bony bump on the top of its head, paleontologists think this was used as a battering ram to fight against other dinosaurs—like how goats headbutt each other.

Ankylosaurus
had a bony club at the end of its tail. It ate plants and used the club to attack any predators who came up behind it while it was eating.

Maiasaura
fossils have been found in a colony of nests, where some eggs had hatched. It seems that the hatchlings stayed living in the nest until they were able to leave and look after themselves. The group of nests shows that Maiasaura lived in herds.

Huge numbers of footprints found in North America show that some dinosaurs traveled in groups and migrated from place to place.

Stegosaurus

Think like a paleontologist!
Look at each of these dinosaurs and write
down what you think they are doing.

Iguanodon

Stegosaurus

I think this dinosaur is _____

_____ because _____

_____.

Iguanodon

I think these dinosaurs are _____

_____ because _____

_____.

Struthiomimus

I think this dinosaur is _____

_____ because _____

_____.

Struthiomimus

17

DINOSAUR RECORD BREAKERS

Paleontologists have discovered many different types of dinosaurs, so we know they come in all shapes and sizes. Here are some of the record breakers—but remember: there's always a chance we will discover a new kind of fossil that will break another record!

Because it's rare for complete skeletons to be found, paleontologists have to make clever guesses about how long or heavy a dinosaur would have been. These records are really good estimates but we can't be completely certain.

The **longest** dinosaur was **Argentinosaurus**, which was 35 meters long (as long as four fire engines!).

The **heaviest** dinosaur was also **Argentinosaurus**!

The **strangest** dinosaur might have been the **Therizinosaurus**—it had long arms and three fingers with claws as long as a man's arm!

One of the **oldest** dinosaurs is **Saltopus**, which lived 245 million years ago. Its fossils have only been found in Scotland.

The **cleverest** dinosaur is thought to be **Troodon** because it had the largest brain relative to the size of its body. It was a clever hunter and paleontologists think it would have had good vision for hunting.

Follow the wiggly line to find out which dinosaur was the fastest!

Answer on page 31.

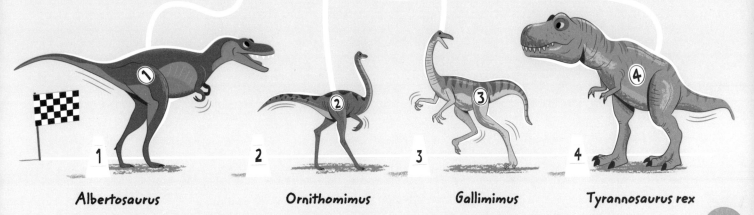

1 Albertosaurus

2 Ornithomimus

3 Gallimimus

4 Tyrannosaurus rex

LIVING FOSSILS

The last of the dinosaurs died out 65 million years ago. However, some species alive today are close relatives of animals and plants we know from fossils, and look very similar. They are called living fossils because they are so closely related to the fossil species. Even though they aren't exactly the same species, they can tell us a lot about how the fossil species lived.

Ginkgo trees grew around half the world in the Jurassic and Cretaceous periods. Now they are native to China and can live for a very long time—some have been alive for 2,500 years!

Horseshoe crabs are not really crabs at all—they are more related to spiders than crabs—but fossils of horseshoe crabs have been found that are 310 million years old!

Coelacanth fish go back 410 million years and were thought to have gone extinct 66 million years ago. However, in 1938 a living coelacanth was found off the coast of South Africa. The species is critically endangered but still alive.

Crocodiles are reptiles that first appeared in the Cretaceous period, 80 million years ago.

Paleontologists believe that birds are descended from dinosaurs. Fossils have been found of dinosaurs covered in feathers like birds!

Spot the ten differences between these two pictures of a living fossil museum.
Answers on page 31.

HUMAN FOSSILS

Fossils have helped us to understand the story of humans too. Modern humans have been around for over 300,000 years but paleontologists have found fossils of many different species of our ancient ancestors. Scientists use the fossils to work out how humans evolved over hundreds of thousands of years.

Scientists compare the shape of our ancient ancestors' bones to the skeletons of humans and gorillas and chimpanzees today to see whether the bones suit walking upright or on all-fours, or climbing trees.
The shape of teeth tells us what sort of food they ate: big molars and powerful jaws are good for grinding up tough meat and plants, while modern humans have less powerful teeth because our food is cooked and easier to eat.

Back curved in an S-shape and wide hips make it easier to walk upright.

A strong thumb that can move independently makes it possible to hold and move things precisely.

Scientists have also learned a lot about ancient humans from the stone tools that have been discovered. Match each of these stone tools to their correct shadow.

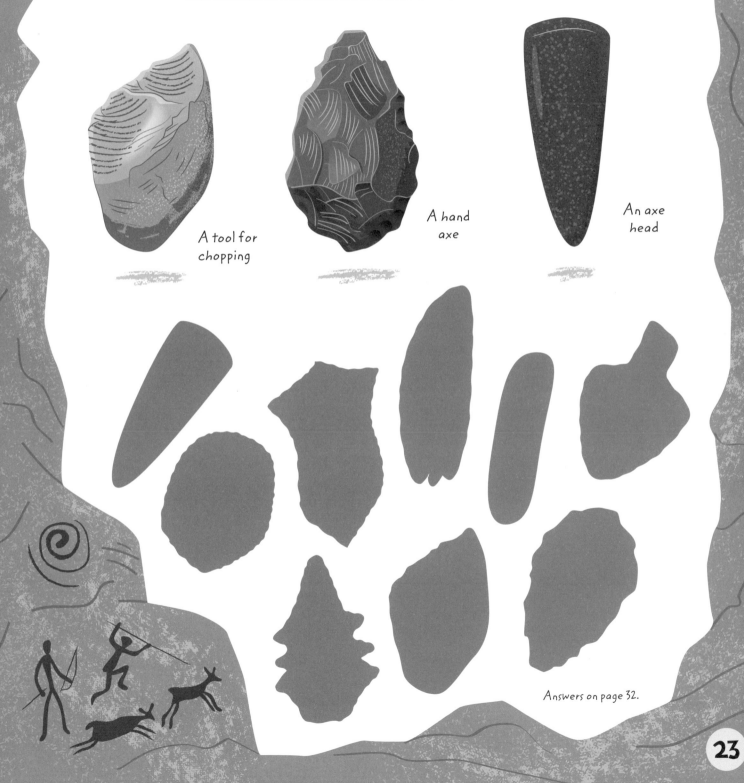

A tool for chopping

A hand axe

An axe head

Answers on page 32.

ANCIENT CLIMATE CLUES

How can we know what the climate was like in the time of dinosaurs? The weather can't be fossilized but the climate can leave clues in the fossils of plants and animals that were alive at the time.

One clue scientists use is in fossilized teeth from extinct animals called "conodonts." The temperature during the life of the conodonts affects the chemicals found in their teeth. Measuring the way the chemicals changed over millions of years tells us how the temperature changed.

Some plant and animal fossils look similar to species alive today, so scientists use what they know of the climate these species like to live in to work out what it was like back then. For example, where fossils of ferns are found, scientists assume the climate was not too cold or too hot.

Triassic

We know that in the Triassic period (252 to 201 million years ago) the land was hot and dry with huge deserts. Lots of volcanoes were erupting, pumping out greenhouse gases that warmed the atmosphere. There were few plants and no flowers. More fossils from this time are found in land that was at the North or South Pole because it was too hot for much to live in the tropics.

Jurassic

The weather in the Jurassic period (201 to 145 million years ago) was milder than in the Triassic, so more plants grew and rainforests took over from deserts.

Cretaceous

The Earth gradually cooled through the Cretaceous period (145 to 66 million years ago), and the first flowers appeared. These included magnolias, passion flowers and buttercups, which are still flowering today!

Follow the clues to find the right dinosaur living in each period.

1. I lived in the Cretaceous, when there were so many different kinds of plants for me to eat. My mouth is shaped like a duck's bill, which helps me eat all the tough but tasty bits from the conifer trees. I love the bark, pine cones, and even the needles!

2. I lived in the Jurassic. We dinosaurs ruled the Earth! With my long neck, I can reach the juicy leaves at the top of trees that other dinosaurs can't get to.

3. I lived in the Triassic. About the size of a car, with slender and muscly legs, I move quickly to grab the small animals I like to eat.

Answers on page 32.

Brachiosaurus

T. rex

Herrerasaurus

Caudipteryx

Pterosaur

Corythosaurus

HOAXES!

When scientists find a new fossil, it can take time to work out what species it is. Sometimes paleontologists make mistakes at first, but over time more scientists work out better ideas about the fossil.

There are also people who try to present a fake fossil as something that has never been seen before. They create something, hoping to fool the public or even scientists—and sometimes it works!

Which of these dinosaur facts are true and which are hoaxes?

Answers on page 32.

T. rex liked to eat stegosaurus.

Some dinosaurs could fly.

Iguanodons had a spike on their nose.

All dinosaurs had claws.

Piltdown Man

In 1912, an English archaeologist called Charles Dawson claimed to have found the skull of a species thought to be a "missing link" between humans and apes, near a village called Piltdown in the UK. It was nearly 40 years before scientists realised the bones were not old enough to be an ancient extinct ape. Looking more closely, they found the bones were actually a mixture of human and orangutan bones, and the teeth had been filed down to look human.

Mixed-up species

When fossils are dug up by farmers or other people who aren't experts, the bones of different species might easily get mixed up. When paleontologists eventually get to see the fossils, the collection of bones can be confusing. This happened in 1999 when people were excited to see a newly discovered fossil of an animal that seemed to have the arms and body of a bird but the tail of a dinosaur. It was named Archaeoraptor, but it turned out that this fossil was actually made up from bones of two completely different animals—a bird and a dinosaur!

All dinosaurs had scaly skin.

Dinosaurs lived in herds.

Diplodocuses laid their eggs while walking.

Whales lived at the same time as dinosaurs.

FUTURE FOSSILS

What kind of fossils might the paleontologists of the future find and learn about us, living today?

Fossils are only made in very particular situations so most things alive today will not end up as a fossil in thousands of years. However, there are lots of things that humans have made that might last for thousands of years, even if they are buried deep underground.

Think about all the things that humans throw away and what they say about us. The different things found in different layers of rock will give clues to what we liked to eat at different times. Around the world, we throw away the bones of 60 billion chickens each year so the rocks formed with today's trash could be full of chicken bones. In the 1800s in London, UK, the story was different: oysters were the popular and cheap food. Today, oyster shells are often found underground or washed up alongside the river.

Write or draw some of the items you think could be discovered in the future. What might they say about us and the way we live?

ANSWERS

page 9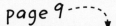

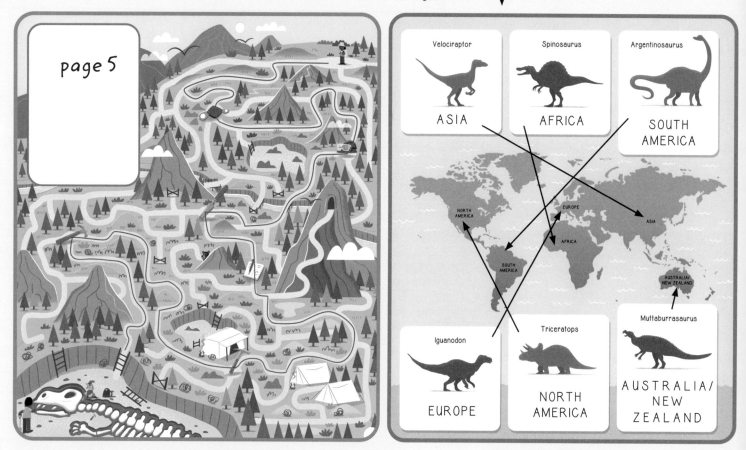

page 5

Velociraptor — ASIA

Spinosaurus — AFRICA

Argentinosaurus — SOUTH AMERICA

Iguanodon — EUROPE

Triceratops — NORTH AMERICA

Muttaburrasaurus — AUSTRALIA/ NEW ZEALAND

pages 10-11

1. C
2. B
3. D
4. A

page 15

y	f	o	s	s	a	g	l	f	e
k	t	k	l	t	y	i	l	r	t
c	y	a	n	r	s	a	r	u	r
a	r	a	t	s	c	n	a	i	i
b	h	b	o	m	i	n	i	y	l
t	y	f	u	s	b	i	r	e	r
d	n	d	e	e	w	a	e	s	u
n	i	n	m	a	s	i	t	u	s
f	o	t	x	o	s	h	c	r	r
l	g	h	r	t	r	k	a	v	t
e	n	i	d	i	o	b	o	p	o
w	a	c	p	c	m	d	n	z	r
a	t	m	s	o	a	e	c	c	t
e	h	t	z	s	t	v	a	q	o
s	a	t	a	j	o	i	y	o	t
m	t	m	r	v	l	a	c	x	u
a	e	q	u	a	i	r	r	a	b
h	r	h	y	t	t	k	j	d	u
i	s	o	d	e	e	o	m	i	s
t	r	i	l	o	b	i	t	e	r
q	s	b	d	r	i	m	e	p	m

page 19

page 21

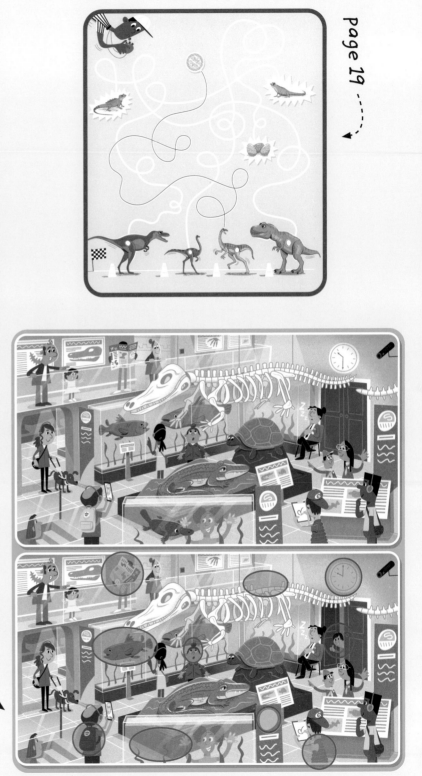

page 23

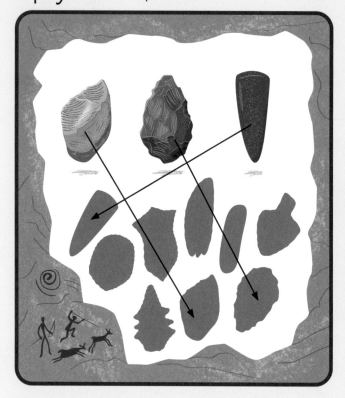

page 25

1. Corythosaurus
2. Brachiosaurus
3. Herrerasaurus

pages 26-27

Iguanodons had a spike on their nose.

FALSE—the spike was on their thumb (but Victorian scientists first thought the spike went on the nose).

T. rex liked to eat stegosaurus.

FALSE—although T. rex liked to eat plant-eating dinosaurs, stegosaurus died out about 80 million years before T. rex evolved!

All dinosaurs had claws.

TRUE

Dinosaurs had scaly skin.

TRUE—even though some dinosaurs may have had feathers as well, their skin was scaly like a lizard's.

Some dinosaurs could fly.

FALSE—dinosaurs all lived on land and while there were flying reptiles that lived at the same time, they weren't dinosaurs.

Dinosaurs lived in herds.

TRUE—fossilized footprints of lots of the same feet show that some dinosaurs moved together in big groups.

Diplodocuses laid their eggs while walking.

TRUE—probably! Diplodocus eggs have been found in lines rather than nests, so they might have popped out while the adult was walking.

Whales lived at the same time as dinosaurs.

FALSE—but when cetiosaurus fossils were first found, people thought it must be related to the whale because their backbones looked similar.